A COLOURING BOOK FOR OAPS

by
John Edward Parsons
2023

CATALOGING INFORMATION
ISBN: 979-886602-435-3
CREDITS
Production Design: Global Wordsmiths

Why?

Well, why not? At eighty-three years of age, creating these drawings and making them into a colouring book for me and others like me seemed like a good idea. As you go through the pages, I hope you'll have a good laugh, as many of my friends did when they saw the finished drawings. You may notice a drawing of a gardener with a carrot in his hand: that's me! My wife is also on that drawing.

One or two of my sketches are a little risqué. Hopefully, most of you won't be upset about that. Motorised scooters with modifications are a big in this book. A lot of those ideas came from other folk of my age—we're all in the same boat, you see.

I should thank my wife, Jennifer, who has given so much time to the birthing of this colouring book. What would I do without her?

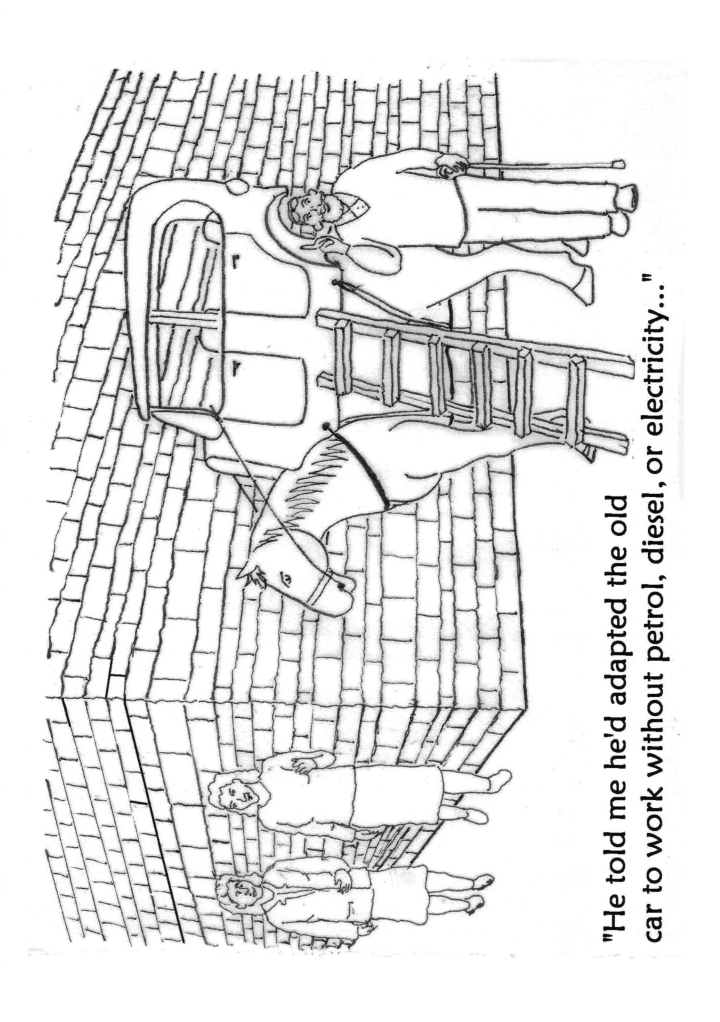

"He told me he'd adapted the old car to work without petrol, diesel, or electricity..."

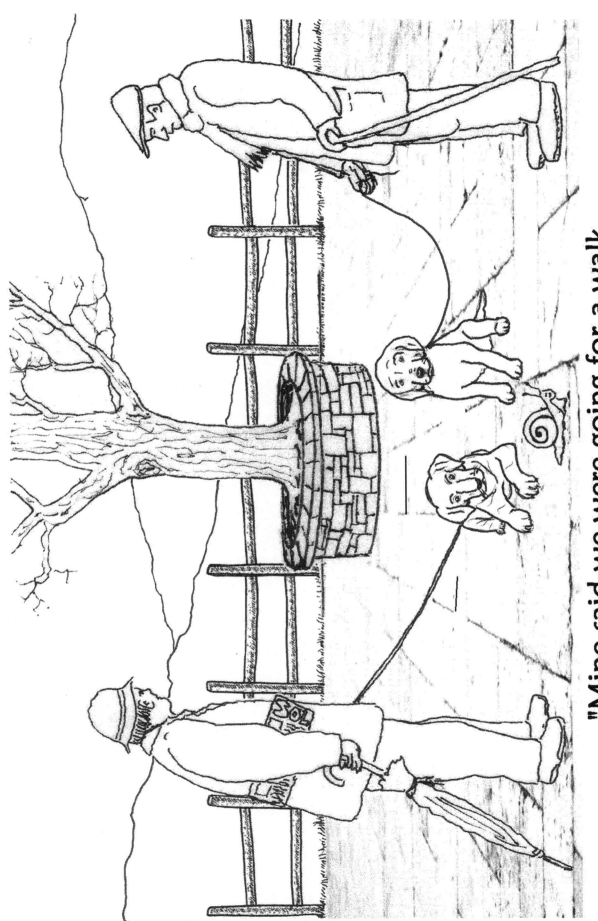

"Mine said we were going for a walk, but it's embarrassing when a snail overtakes you!"

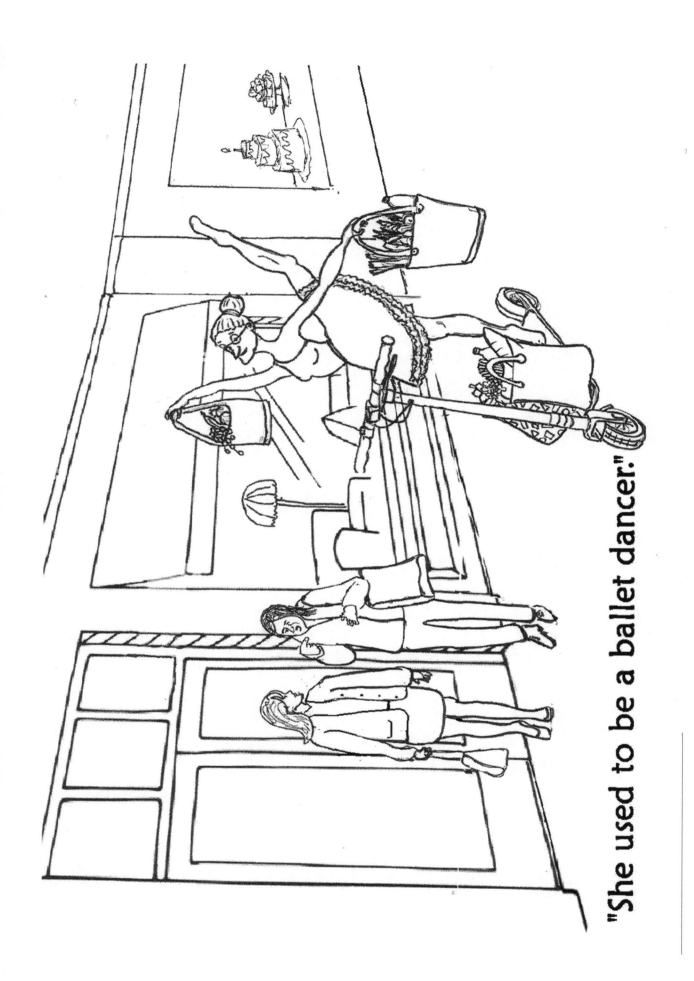

"She used to be a ballet dancer."

"You're displaying all your credentials, Maud!
Wait for the steps to get into the basket."

"What a big one you've got there, John."

"That's the first time you've said that to me for ages, Jennifer."

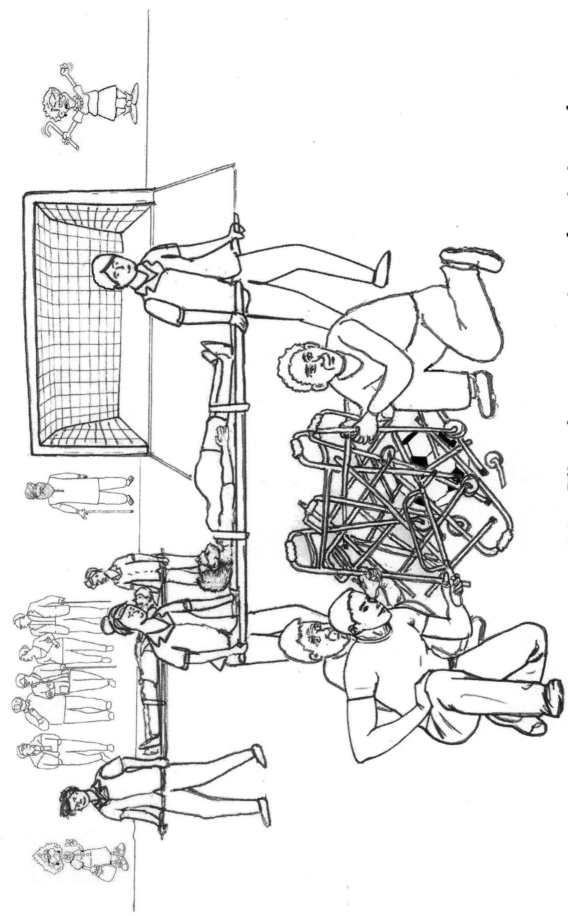

"It was a Zimmer tackle. They're removing the injured while they sort out the Zimmers to get the ball."

He used to be a bus driver.

"Oh, Grandad, you're supposed to *blow* the candles out, not knock them down."

"He always puts her in the caravan. It's the only way he can turn the sat nav off."

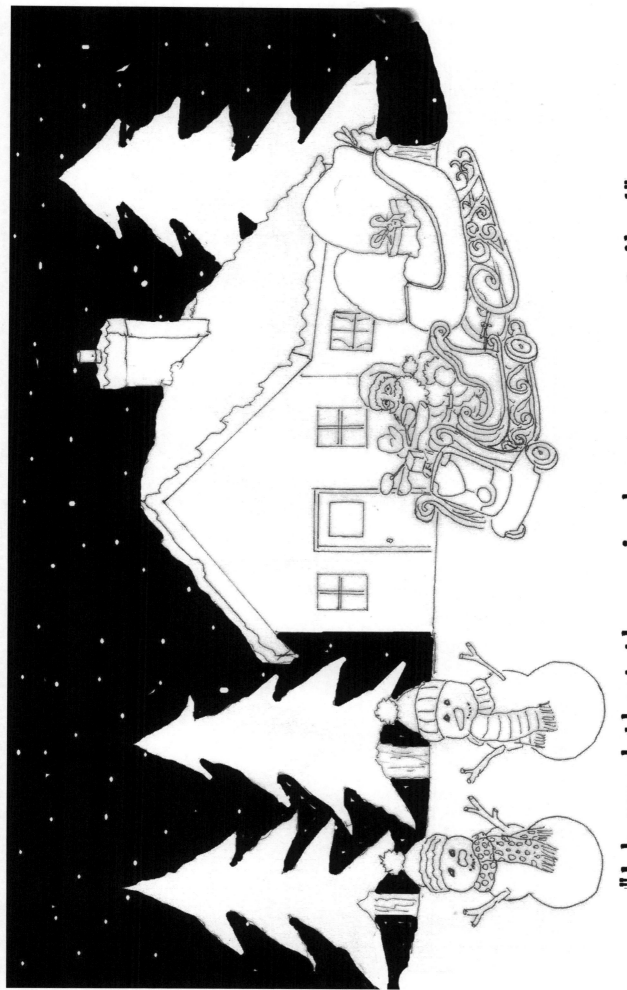

"I heard that the reindeer are on strike!"

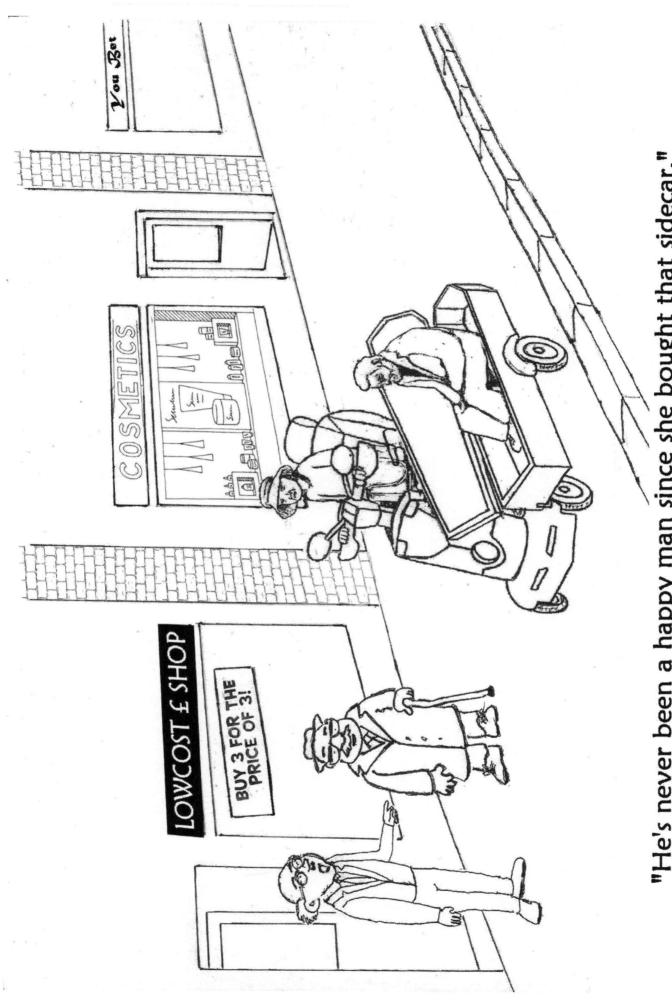

"He's never been a happy man since she bought that sidecar."

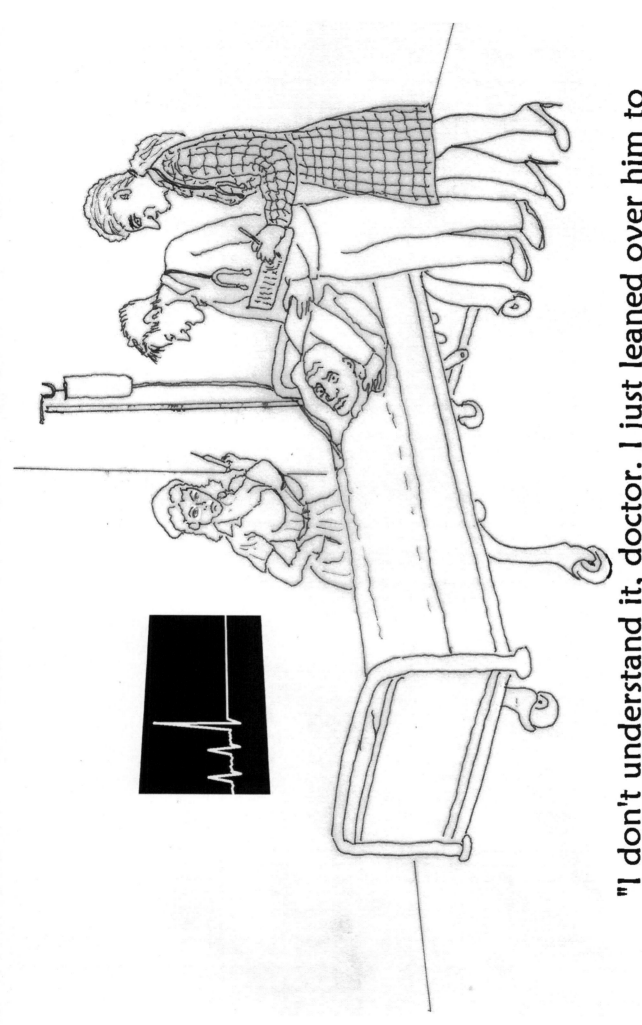

"I don't understand it, doctor. I just leaned over him to give him his injection, and his eyes bulged and he died."

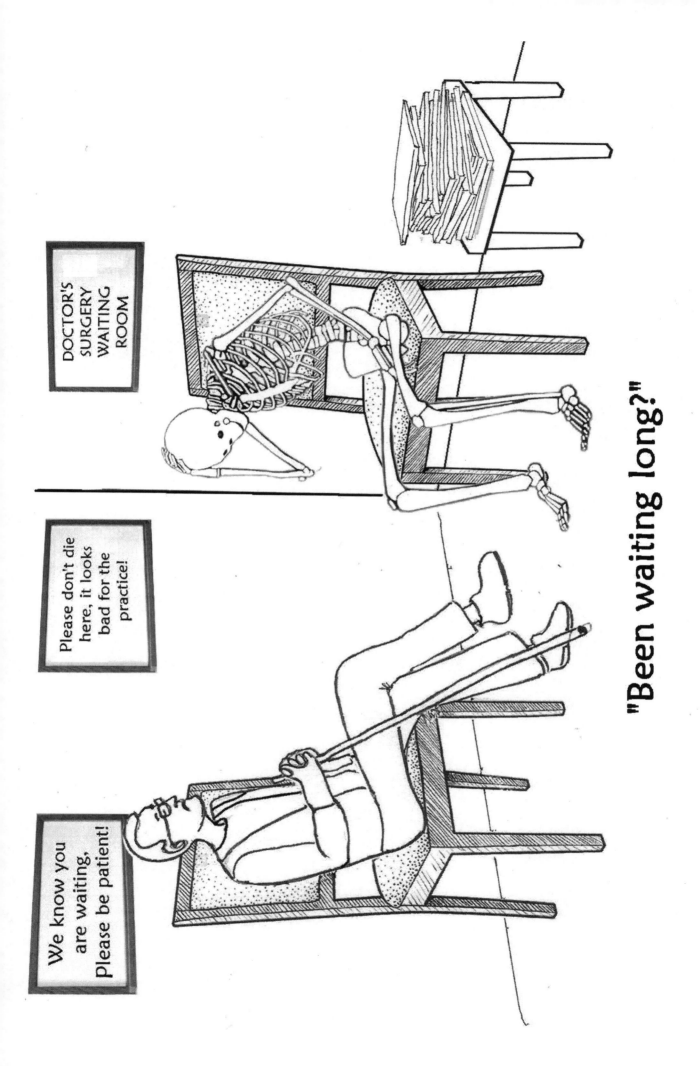

"Now, you go with the nice man for a walk, and I will see you back here later."

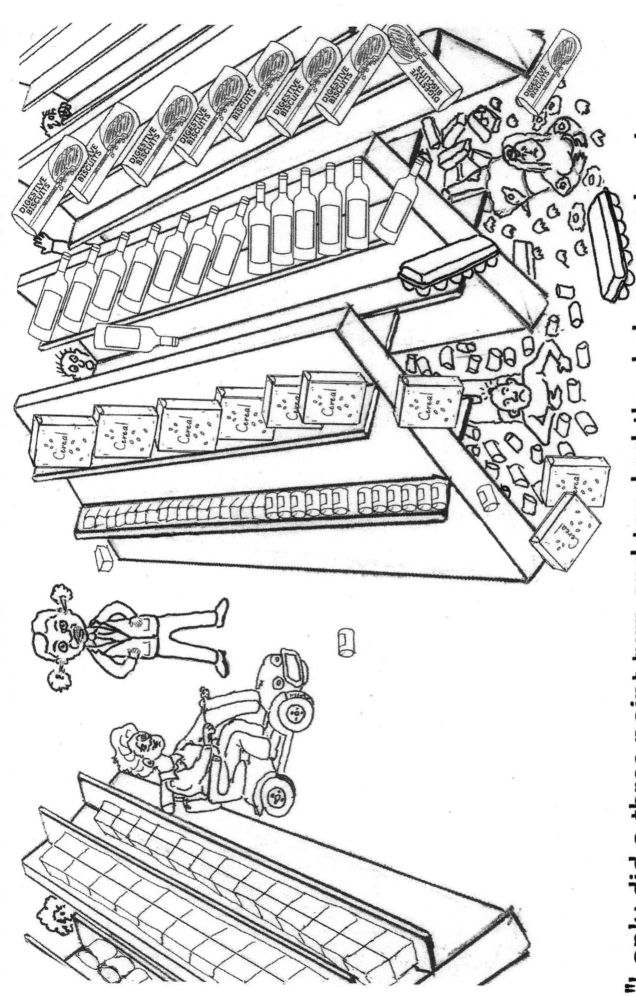

"I only did a three point turn and touched the shelves, so what damage other than the tin on the floor did I do?"

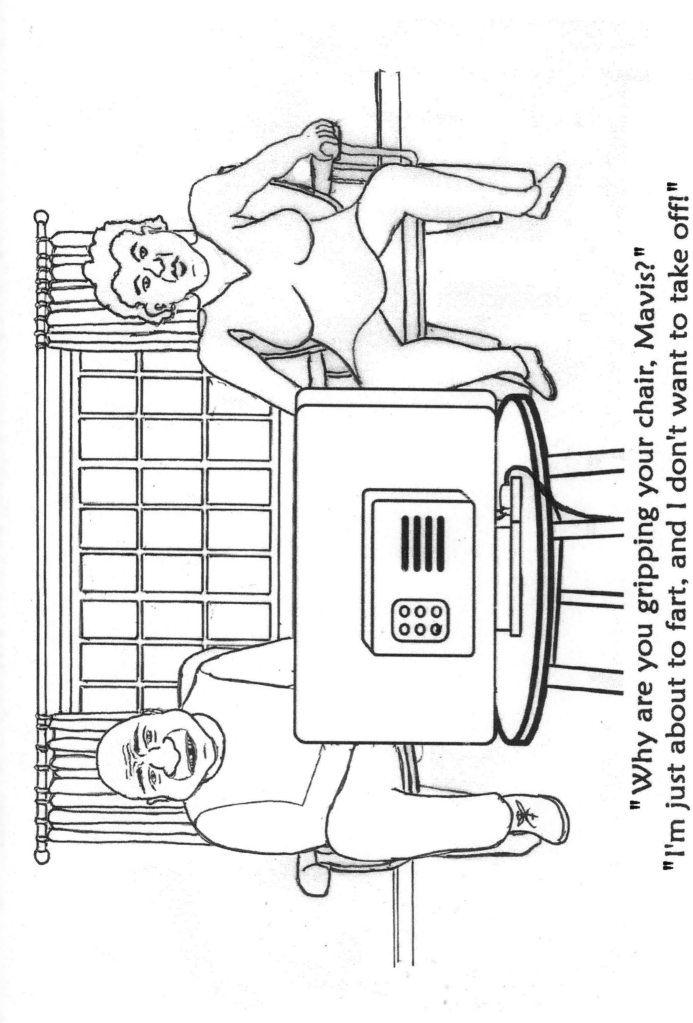

"Why are you gripping your chair, Mavis?"
"I'm just about to fart, and I don't want to take off!"

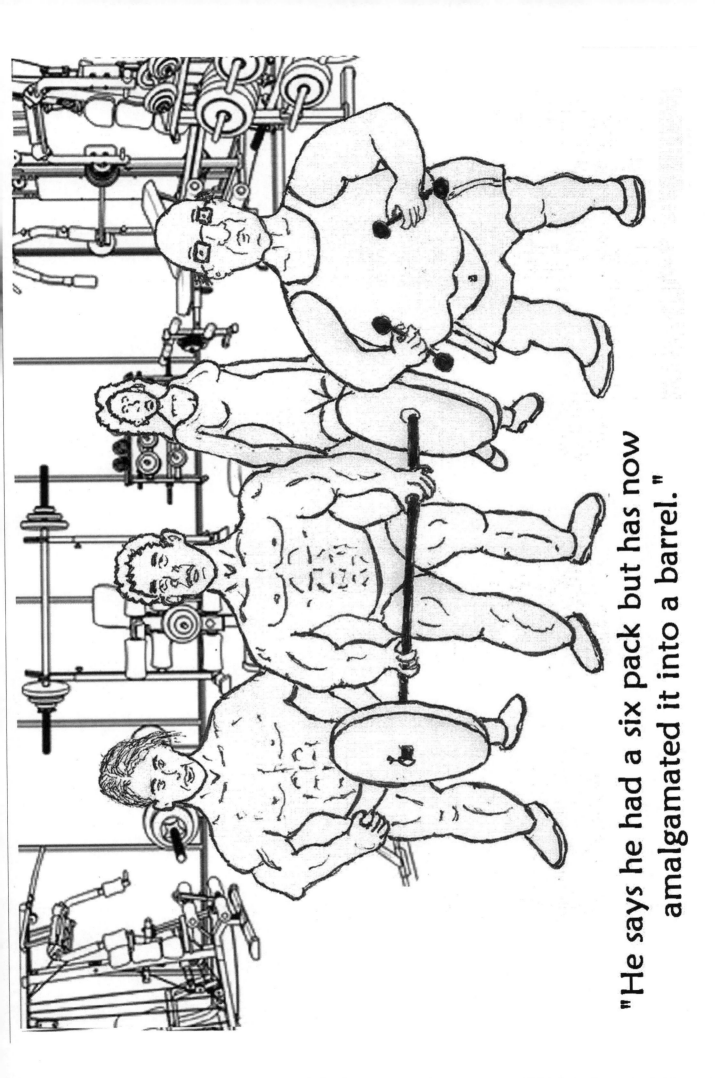

"He says he had a six pack but has now amalgamated it into a barrel."

"Grandpa fixed an umbrella to his scooter; the wind came and took him up there. We're waiting for him to come down."

"There goes Mavis with her week's supply of shopping!"

It's all go, gardening!

"He couldn't afford hearing aids so he made his own."

AUDIOLOGIST

Our hearing aids are neat and small.

We are not ear today and gone tomorrow.

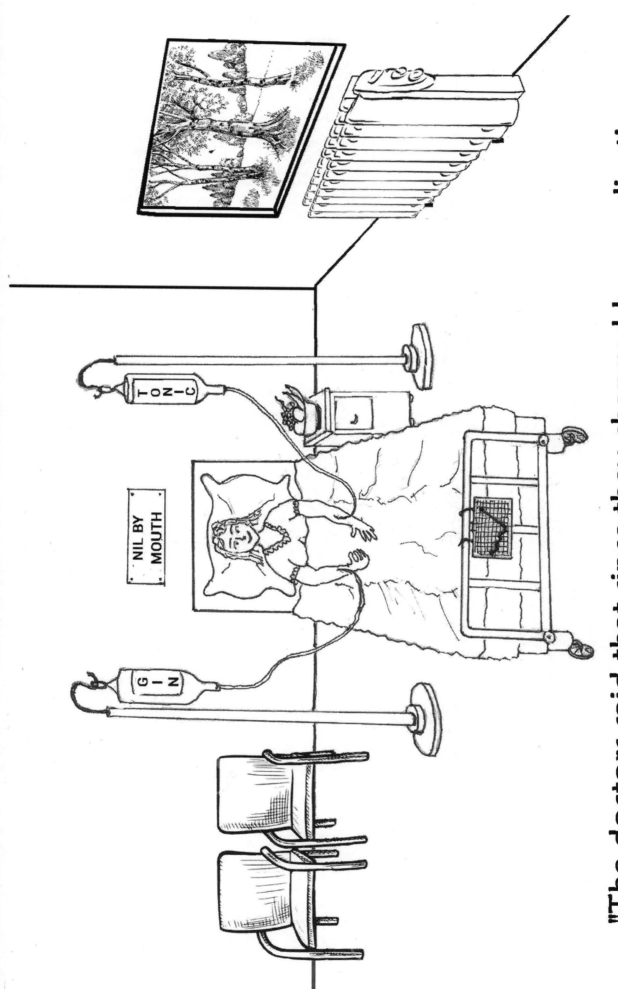

"The doctors said that since they changed her medication, she's made a remarkable recovery!"

"Claude was an inventor, and it looks as if he still is!"

"That'll teach you. Next time, don't call me a silly old fart!"

"He used to be a lorry driver."

"George, I think we're lost..."

"He couldn't afford a motorised scooter."

"You're panting like a dog again. Try to remember, she will look like me in sixty years' time."

"Have you noticed how dog owners begin to look like their animals?"

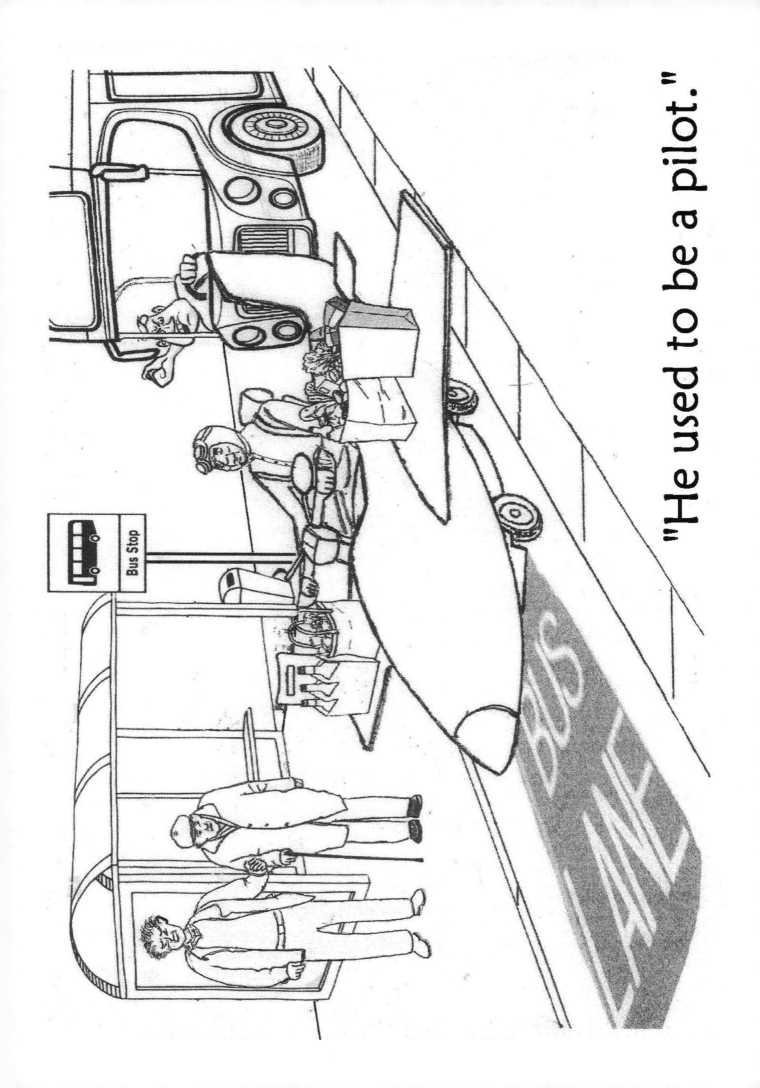

"He used to be a pilot."

"Another one lost, sergeant. Shall I put her in the lost and found pen, until she's claimed?"

"I don't care who you are! You can't park on double yellow lines!"

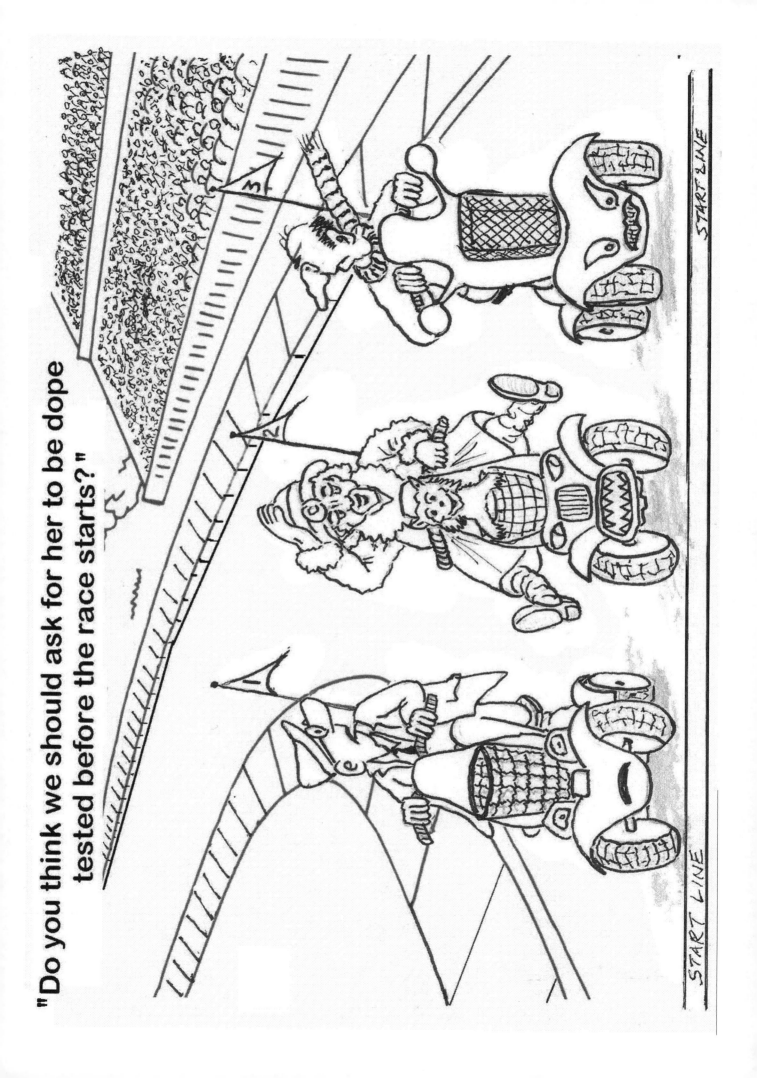

"Some healthy exercise for the residents clearing the snow makes a lot of sense."

"George, your pets have got out again and are upsetting our guests."

"Look, George, I'm swimming with dolphins!"

"Grandma, there are sheep on your lawn."

"Yes, dear, it's Grandad's idea; they mow the lawn as they fertilise it."

"He used to be a deep sea fisherman."

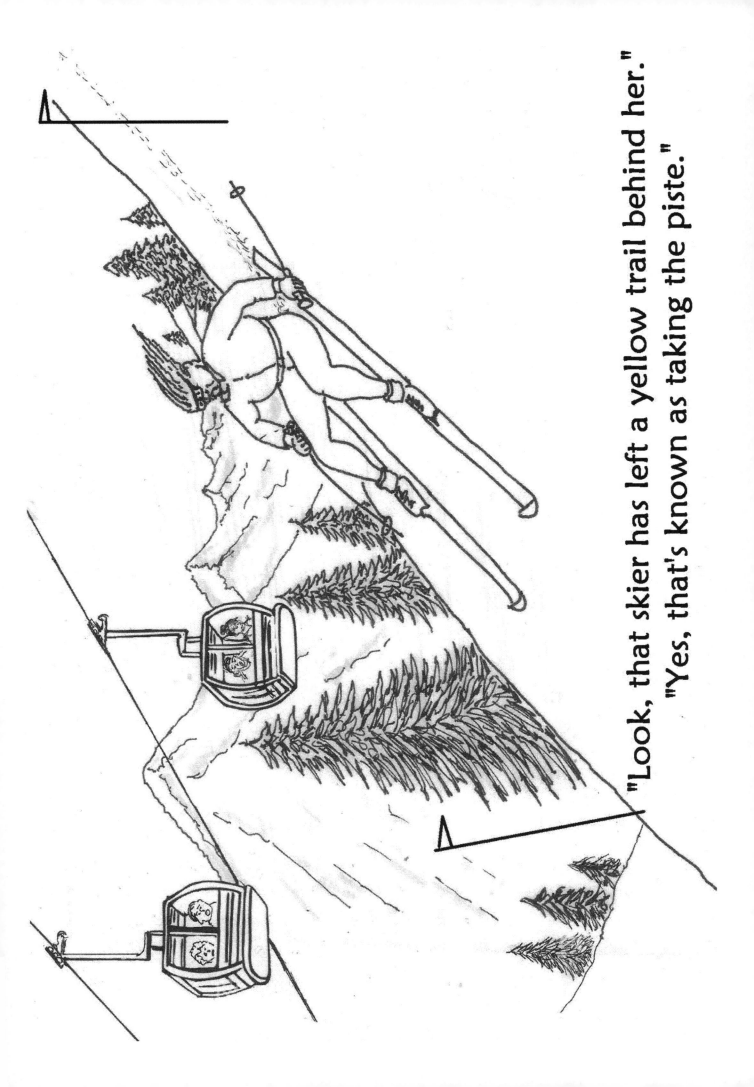

"Look, that skier has left a yellow trail behind her."
"Yes, that's known as taking the piste."

"No, constable, I wasn't going 90 MPH or causing an accident. I'm an OAP. We don't do anything fast!"

"These motorised scooters are much more
fun than my old broom!"

"I have no intention of spilling it!"

"She likes to build snowmen; it gives her fond memories."

"Four aces and a king. Mary, you're either very very lucky or you're cheating."

"He used to be a submariner."

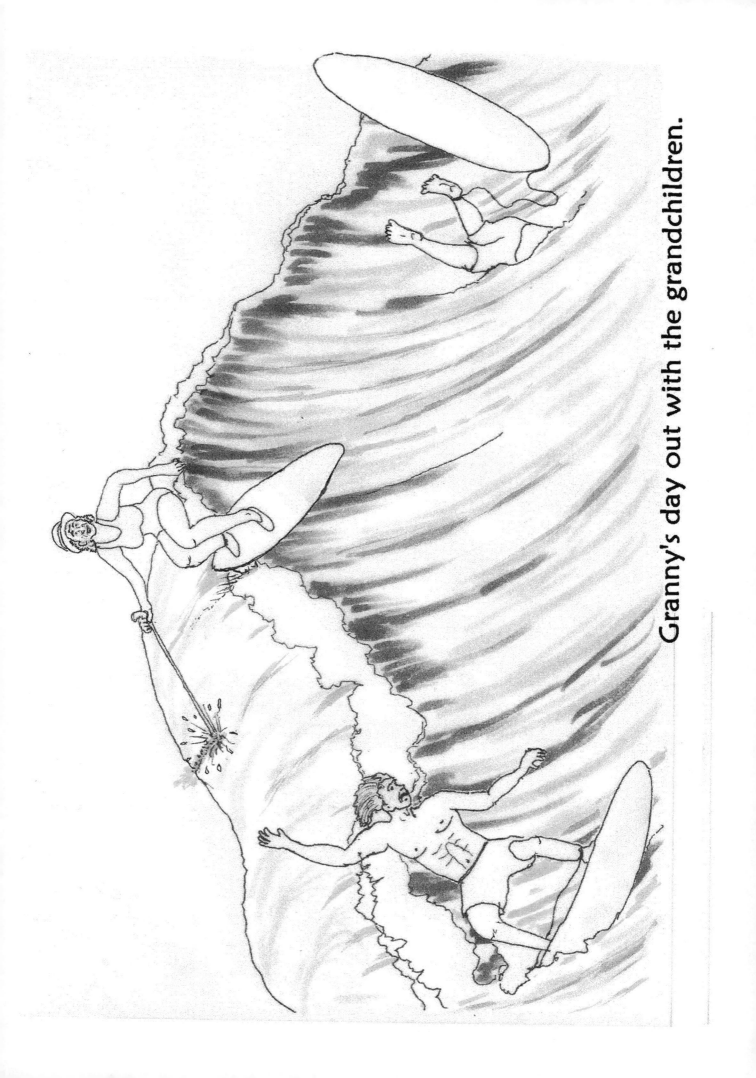

Granny's day out with the grandchildren.

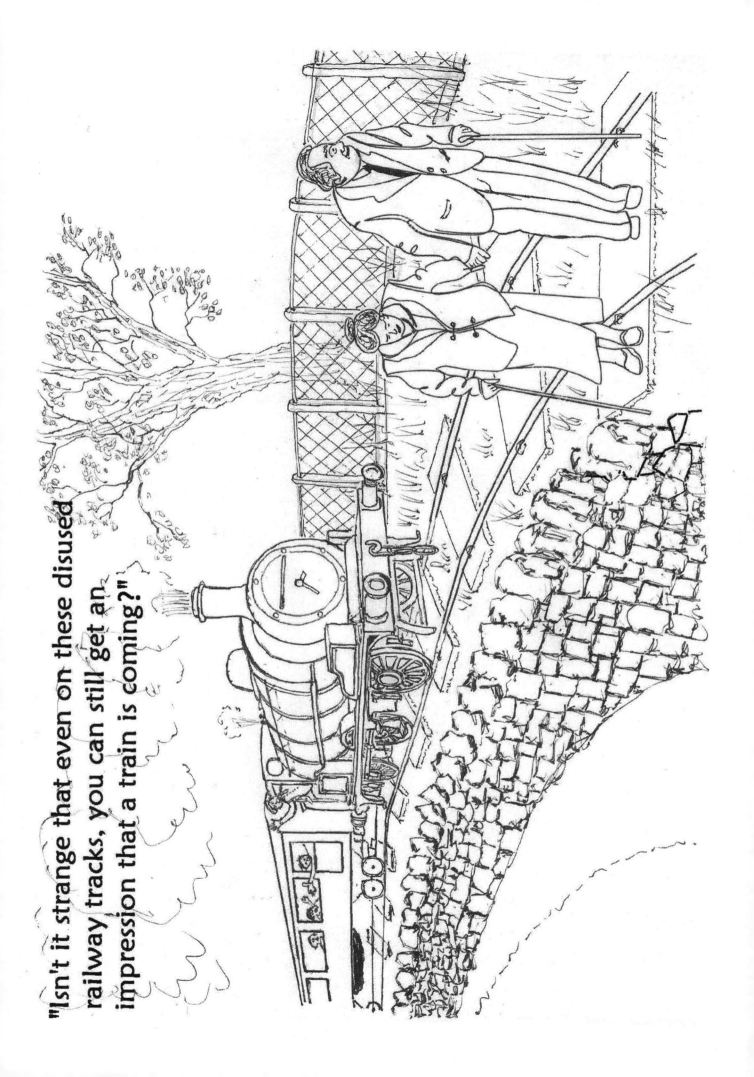

"Isn't it strange that even on these disused railway tracks, you can still get an impression that a train is coming?"

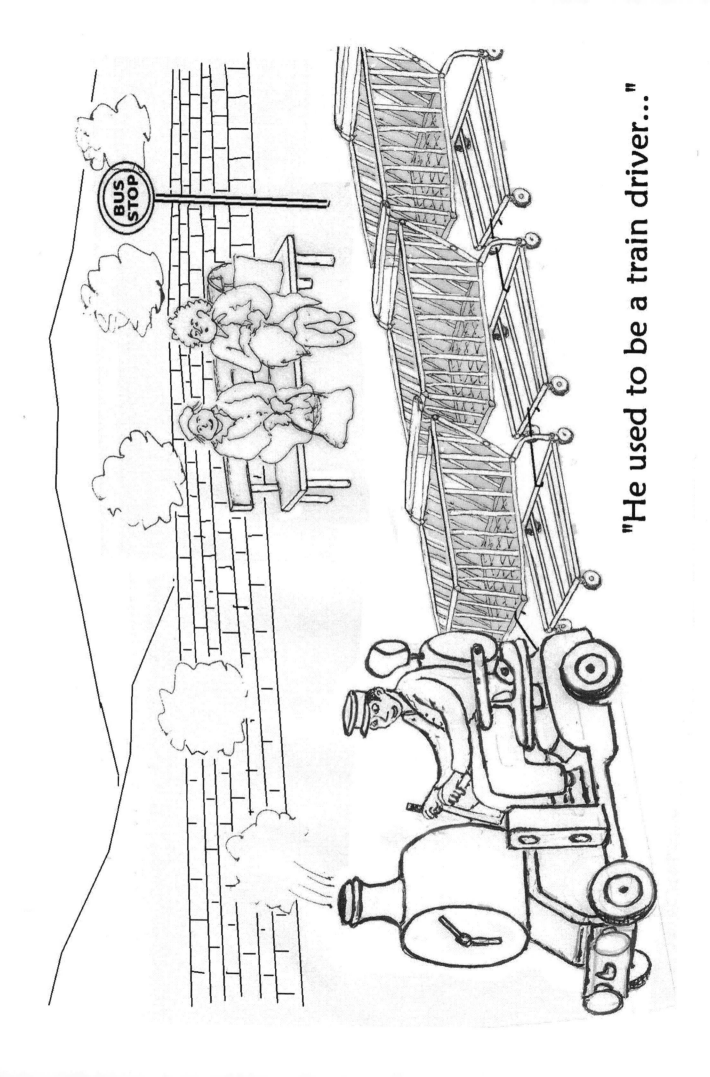

"He used to be a train driver..."

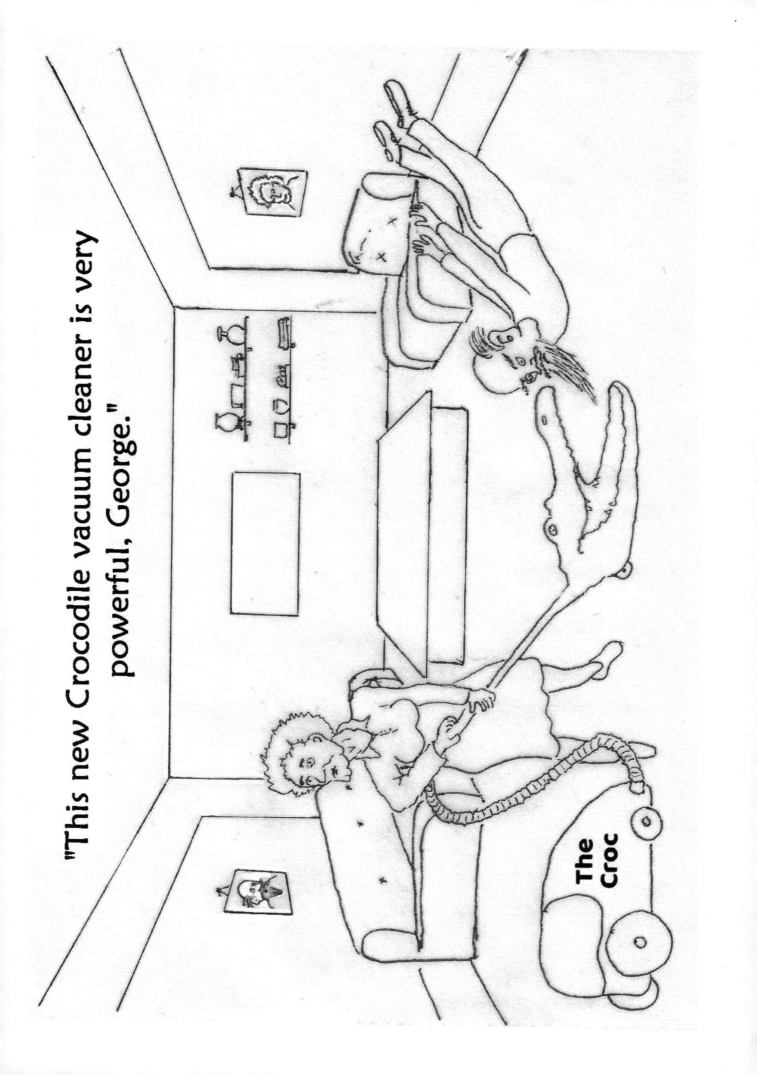

"He used to be a stretch limousine driver..."

"Wendy, have you seen my pet anaconda? It's not in its cage."

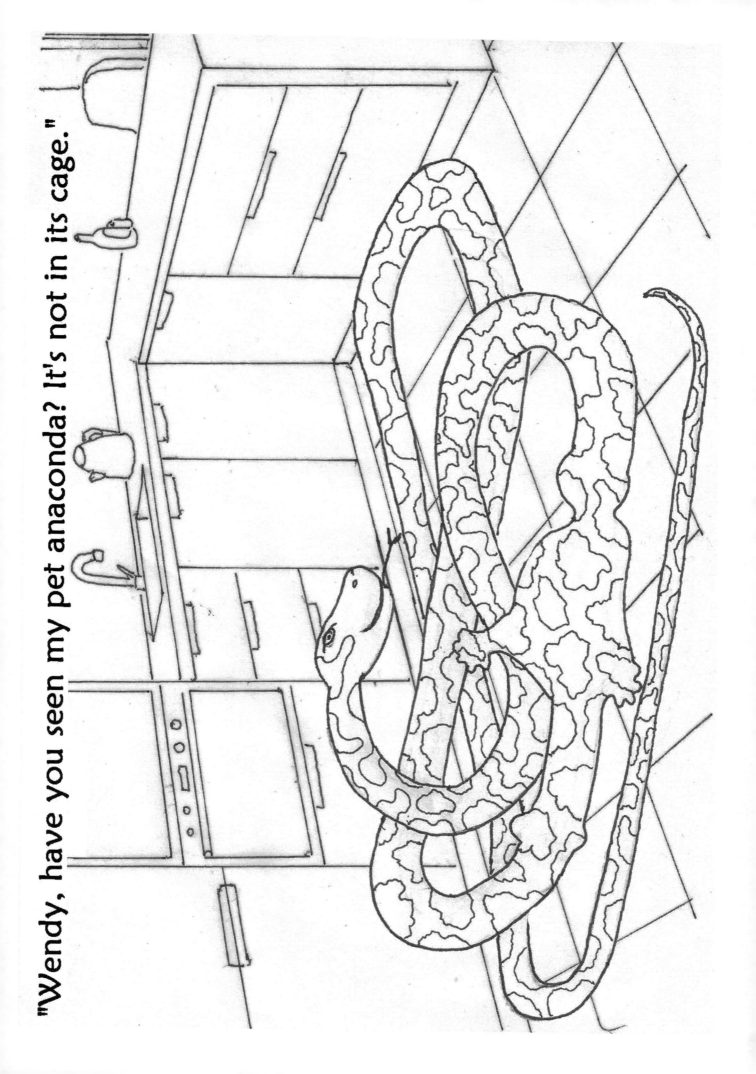

"I told Gillian to go on on down to the greenhouse to look at your strange plant..."

"He used to be a car mechanic..."

"So, it *is* true."

These are a children's series of five books. Travel with Scott, our hero, who wanders through worlds created by wizards and witches. Each book is a standalone story, with slight references to the past books. Priced at £8.99, they're available through Amazon.

These last few pages are my other books, all reading books with drawings in the children's books. They're all available from Amazon, save but one. Rose the dancer can only be purchased through me.

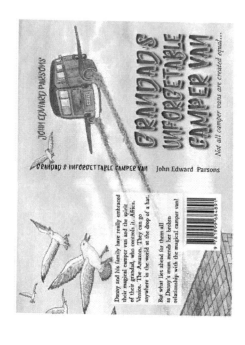

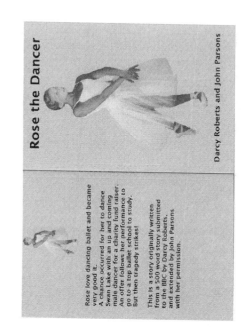

Printed in Great Britain
by Amazon

45252375R00073